Revitalizing the Retail Trade Sector in Rural Communities: Lessons from Three Midwestern States

by:

Janet S. Ayres
Department of Agricultural Economics
Purdue University

F. Larry Leistritz
Department of Agricultural Economics
North Dakota State University

Kenneth E. Stone
Department of Economics
Iowa State University

North Central Regional Center for Rural Development

November 1992
RRD 162

November 1992
Library of Congress Catalog Card Number: 92-62079
ISBN 0-936913-05-3

RRD 162 is available from:
North Central Regional Center for Rural Development
216 East Hall
Iowa State University
Ames, IA 50011
(515) 294-8321

Printed by University Publications
Iowa State University

Contents

List of Tables

List of Figures

List of Appendix Tables

Executive Summary

The loss of retail businesses and sales in rural areas has been evolving for many years. Improved roads and interstates, the proliferation of automobiles, the lure of shopping malls and discount stores in urban areas, and consumer preferences for greater selection and lower prices in merchandise are some of the reasons that rural communities find it difficult to compete.

This study identified 37 rural communities in Indiana, Iowa and North Dakota that appeared to have better-than-average retail sales to determine their common characteristics and operational methods. In general, the aim of the study was to identify successful strategies employed by communities and individual businesses. Specifically, the study examined the current status of rural retail communities; identified organizational techniques to promote retail sales and businesses; examined effective business funding techniques and recruitment approaches to bring new businesses to the community; identified successful promotional campaigns; and determined the most critical needs of rural business communities.

The study was conducted in two phases. The first phase involved examination of rural sales through state sales tax records and other sources, and a survey of town clerks in all towns with a population between 500 and 5,000 in the three states. The data from this phase were used to determine the more "successful" communities in retail sales and business performance. Towns for further study were selected from three population substrata (i.e., populations of 500-999; 1,000-2,499; and 2,500-5,000) and from different areas of the respective states. Thirty-seven communities were chosen for further study.

The second phase involved in-depth interviews in each of the study communities. County extension agents were typically the first point of contact and they, along with town clerks and mayors, were instrumental in identifying community officials, business proprietors, and other community leaders who could best provide information regarding the local business climate, recruitment and promotional strategies and related topics.

The findings revealed that developing or maintaining a healthy retail sector in a rural community is an up-hill battle. The turn-over and change in the business community was constant in the study areas. One of the struggles for the local leaders is the ability to deal with this constant change.

A second observation was that there is no "ideal" community. While better-than-average retail communities were chosen for this study, they still confronted many problems. Some communities had a relatively strong retail sector, yet were struggling to keep their elementary school or were searching for alternative solutions to solid waste disposal. This reality of small town life reflects, once again, the constant change in communities, the dependency on volunteer leadership to deal with the change, and the limited availability of human and financial resources to assist in community efforts.

A third general finding was the similarity of issues across the three states. It was expected that because of the differences in urbanization and economic base in the states, that differences would be found in rural community issues. However, the concerns and issues expressed by the community leaders were nearly identical.

The findings from the interviews revealed that more successful towns generally have stronger community organizations and better local cooperation. There were strong ties between the business community and local government and with other community groups. The organizations were well organized and had active involvement from the business community. The larger communities were hiring full-time paid professionals to assist them in local economic development efforts. Many of the communities were cooperating with neighboring towns or with the county in order to finance such a position.

The local banks were regarded as the primary source for operating capital for established businesses. Operating capital was not found to be a problem. Capital for new businesses, however, was a major problem as many new businesspeople were undercapitalized and had little or no experience in running a business. Branch banking appeared to have exacerbated the problem as branch bank managers were perceived to have less interest in the community. Transferring the ownership of an existing business to a new owner was found to be as difficult as financing a new business. Although a few creative solutions were found in the study communities, equity financing and long-term debt of new businesses and the transference of a business to new owners remain a problem in most rural communities.

The study communities had very active business recruitment efforts underway to add new basic sector employees to the community and to add to the local retail sector. Frequently, the retail recruitment efforts were aimed at replacing a business that had been lost previously such as an implement dealer, pharmacy or variety store.

Promotional campaigns were used to encourage shopping in the local community. Many events were held around holiday themes or local tourist attractions. The importance of a home-owned newspaper was pointed out as a major asset in promotion. Many businesspeople believed that "word-of-mouth" was their best advertising.

Several critical needs were identified by the business community. The most basic concern requiring communitywide action was the need for economic diversification. Many of the communities are dependent upon a single economic sector, such as agriculture, and the business leaders are now attempting to diversify by attracting new basic employers. Other community issues identified as critical to the retail sector include keeping the school in the community, medical facilities, and the updating/ expansion of the sanitary sewer system. The need for assistance in strategic planning to deal effectively with these issues was evident in many of the communities.

Both business proprietors and community leaders indicated a high level of interest in technical assistance for businesses in the areas of: financial management, business plan development, merchandising, inventory management, personnel management, and customer relations.

In summary, several lessons were learned from this study that have implications for community development practitioners, researchers and policymakers, including: assisting rural communities build a more diversified economic base; providing business management training; establishing mechanisms to transfer established business operations to new owners; developing financing mechanisms for new or aspiring businesses; and assisting rural communities in dealing with change and to plan for their future.

Revitalizing the Retail Trade Sector in Rural Communities: Lessons from Three Midwestern States

Most rural communities have faced hard times during the past decade. The farm crisis, the restructuring of manufacturing, and the decline of mining and other natural resource-based industries have brought economic hardships to many rural communities in the Midwest, as well as in other regions of the country. The rural retail business sector has been hit particularly hard, because small town businesses have typically been capturing a declining share of what has too often been a shrinking market (Stone 1988; Leistritz, Wanzek and Hamm 1990; Johnson and Young 1987). For example, in North Dakota, taxable sales adjusted for inflation decreased 17.9 percent from 1980 to 1987, and the share of total sales captured by towns with less than 10,000 population fell from 36.4 percent in 1980 to 29.8 percent in 1987 (Leistritz et al. 1989).

The relative decline of the rural retail sector can be traced back several decades. For example, in a study conducted for the White House Conference on Small Business, Stone and McConnon (1980) found that rural counties in Iowa, Kansas, Missouri and Nebraska experienced a retail leakage of about 5 percent during the 1950s, 10 percent in the 1960s, and 15 percent in the 1970s. The leakage now averages well over 20 percent for rural counties in Iowa.

A number of factors have contributed to the declining market share of the smaller rural trade centers, beginning with improvements in rural roads and highways, followed by school consolidation (which led to decreased traffic to the towns that lost their schools), television sets in almost every rural home (which increased consumers' exposure to new products and urban shopping centers), and more recently the expansion of urban and suburban malls, shopping centers and discount stores (which are increasingly luring customers out of the rural areas).

Whatever the causes, the effects of declining retail sales volume can be devastating to small towns. In Iowa, during the period 1980-1988, towns with 500 to 1,000 residents had an average decrease in deflated taxable sales of 51.9 percent and towns of 1,500 to 2,500 had a decrease of 32.9 percent, compared to a statewide decrease of 13.7 percent (Appendix Table 1, p. 27). The continual loss of retail sales in small towns translates into loss of businesses. For example, Iowa has experienced a net loss of 605 grocery stores (33 percent) in the last 10 years—most in towns of less than

1

1,000 population. The loss of a key business, such as a grocery store, can be a severe blow to a small town because residents may be forced to travel more frequently to larger towns to shop, and sales of the surviving local stores may suffer. Business closures also eliminate jobs for local residents and reduce the tax base of local governments. Declining employment opportunities may lead to out-migration of local residents, which further erodes the clientele base for Main Street businesses. Thus, the whole process can become a vicious cycle with economic, demographic and public sector decline reinforcing each other (Ekstrom and Leistritz 1988).

While it can be argued that the decline of small towns is simply the result of the market system at work, some rural residents may experience substantial inconvenience as a result. Most notably, the elderly often are not in a position to move to a larger town and are sometimes limited in their ability to travel. Elderly residents comprise a large and growing segment of the rural population. In Iowa, for example, persons over age 65 accounted for 19.7 percent of the 1986 population of counties in which the largest town was less than 2,500. Similarly, this group accounted for 16.7 percent of the 1980 population in North Dakota's agriculturally-dependent counties, up from 13.2 percent in 1970. A relevant question is whether small town residents are destined to forever be isolated from the basic shopping amenities, or whether it is possible for some small towns to maintain a viable business district?

This study was designed to contribute to a better understanding of the dynamics of rural retail trade and to document strategies that have been successfully employed by rural communities to revitalize their retail sectors. The overall goal of the effort was to provide information and insights that will enhance informational programs developed for rural businesspersons and community leaders. Specific objectives include:

1. Determining the recent changes and current status of rural retail communities in Indiana, Iowa and North Dakota.
2. Identifying successful organizational techniques.
3. Identifying innovative and effective business funding techniques.
4. Determining the extent and success of new business recruiting techniques.
5. Identifying successful promotional campaigns based on local resources or factors.
6. Determining the most critical needs common to business communities.

The findings from the study will be disseminated to rural leaders and businesspeople to help them understand the current situation with regard to rural retailing, and thus enable them to develop or maintain the best possible retail business district for their town.

Methods

Because the aim of this study was to identify successful strategies employed by communities and by individual businesses, it was first important to identify communities that had been relatively successful in maintaining or expanding their retail sector. Two major data sources were used in this initial phase. First, data from secondary sources (such as state sales tax records, the *Survey of Buying Power*, and the

1982 and 1987 Retail Business Censuses) were examined to identify the relative retail performance of various towns or counties. Then a survey of town clerks of all towns with populations between 500 and 5,000 was conducted in each of the three states.

The clerks were asked to respond to a questionnaire that contained questions regarding the number of vacant stores, the number of business losses, the dominant stores, and a number of other questions about the community. The town clerks were chosen as the contact point in the communities because every town has a clerk and they are usually very knowledgeable about the community. Also, the mailing list for town clerks was the most accurate community source available. The response to the survey ranged from 71 percent in Indiana to 92 percent in North Dakota. The clerks generally had a good knowledge of the retail situation in their town, but in a few cases they gave the questionnaire to another knowledgeable person (such as the mayor or the Chamber of Commerce president) to complete.

Data from the survey were used along with information on trends in retail sales to identify several communities for more comprehensive study. Most of the communities selected were those that seemed to be among the small retail communities with above-average sales, but a few towns that had experienced below-average retail performance also were included to provide a comparison. Other selection criteria included a desire to select towns from three population substrata (i.e., populations of 500-999; 1,000-2,499; and 2,500-5,000) and from different areas of the respective states. The communities selected for in-depth analysis in Indiana, Iowa and North Dakota are shown in Figures 1, 2 and 3 (pp. 4-6), respectively, and some of their key socioeconomic characteristics are shown in Appendix Tables 2, 3 and 4 (pp. 27-31).

The final step in the study consisted of conducting in-depth interviews in each of the study communities. County extension agents were typically the first point of contact and they, along with town clerks and mayors, were instrumental in identifying community officials, business proprietors, and other community leaders who could best provide information regarding the local business climate, recruitment and promotional strategies, and related topics. Networking techniques (whereby interviewees were asked to suggest other key people to whom the interview team should talk) were also used to expand the contact network. A set of questions was used to guide the interviews. Many of the questions (e.g., concerning recruitment or promotional strategies or a general assessment of the local business climate) were common to all participants, but supplemental questions were added for particular classes of respondents (e.g., bankers and community economic development representatives). Interviews typically required 1 to 1.5 hours to complete. An average of 10 interviews were conducted in each town, with most of the following persons represented:

- Mayor
- Representative of local Chamber of Commerce and/or local economic development corporation
- Proprietors of dominant businesses (as identified by local informants)
- Local banker
- Newspaper and/or radio station representative
- Other community leaders

3

Figure 1. Indiana Cities Selected for In-depth Interviews

4

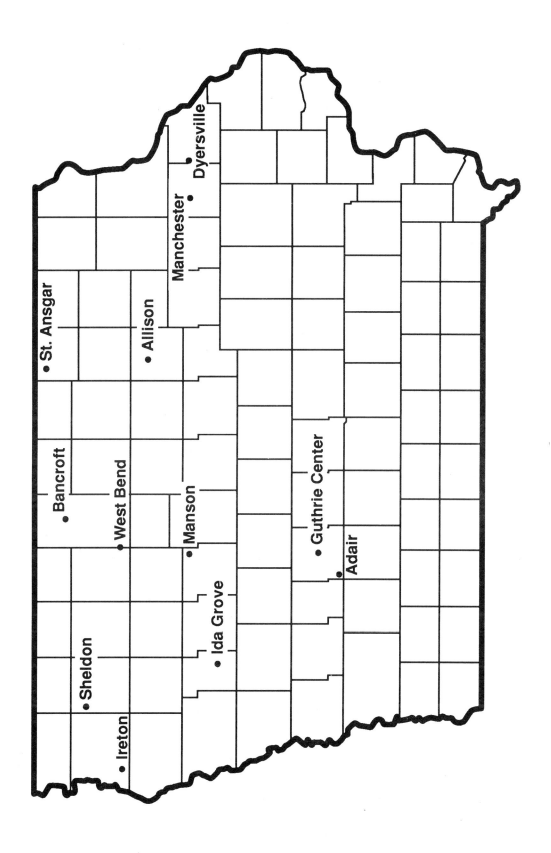

Figure 2. Iowa Cities Selected for In-depth Interviews

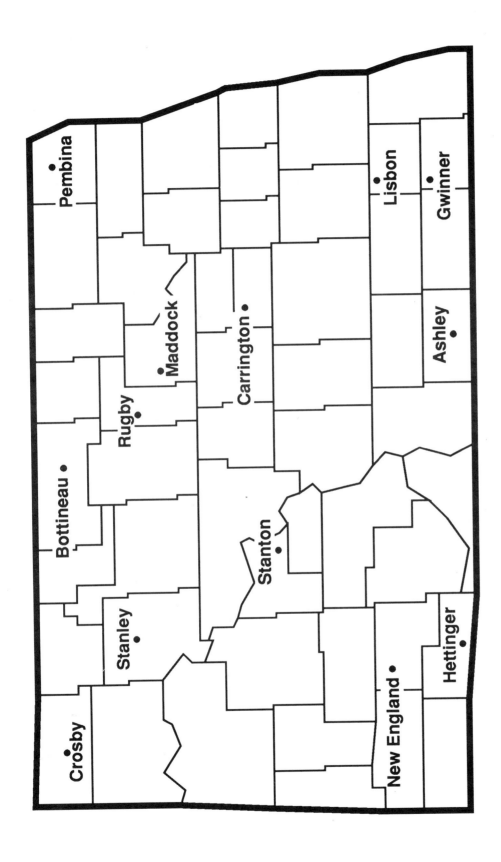

Figure 3. North Dakota Cities Selected for In-depth Interviews

Findings

The major findings of the study are summarized in the sections that follow. First, the findings of the mail survey of town clerks are presented, then the findings of the interviews with community leaders and businesspeople are summarized.

Survey of Town Clerks

The town clerks were asked whether their town had an active organization that promoted retail trade. Most towns had such an organization (Table 1, p. 9), but the larger towns in each state had a higher percentage of reporting an organization.

The clerks were also asked for an overall assessment of how their town's retail sector had been doing in the past few years. Respondents from larger towns were more likely to believe that the retail sector had done fairly well or held its own, while those in the smaller towns were about equally split between those who believed that their retail sector had declined and those who believed it had held its own or improved (Table 2, p. 10).

When asked what types of businesses had done best in their communities, the clerks responded with a wide variety of answers. However, grocery stores were mentioned most frequently by the respondents in each of the three states, followed by restaurants and fast food outlets (Table 3, p. 11). Gasoline and service stations, convenience stores, hardware stores, and farm supply and farm equipment establishments were also frequently mentioned as being among the business types that had done best.

Interestingly, restaurants and fast food establishments and grocery stores were also frequently mentioned when the clerks were asked about the types of businesses that had not done well in their communities (Table 4, p. 12), as were hardware stores. Respondents in communities of 2,500 to 5,000 population most often mentioned clothing stores as a business type experiencing problems.

Town clerks were asked whether their towns had one or more dominant stores that attract customers from beyond the town's normal trade area. Businesses that were frequently mentioned in this regard were farm supply and farm equipment establishments (particularly in smaller towns), grocery stores (especially in the larger towns), eating places and services (such as medical facilities and banks).

An attempt was made to measure the number of retail businesses that had opened and closed in the community during the last three years. The results differed substantially among the states. In Indiana, the smallest towns (populations of 500-999) recorded a net loss of businesses, while the larger towns had net gains. In North Dakota, on the other hand, net losses of businesses (i.e., the number closed exceeded the number opened) were found in all town size groups. Further, the majority of towns in each size group had experienced net losses of businesses.

7

The clerks were also asked about the number of retail building spaces, both occupied and vacant, in their business districts. Although very few towns (e.g., 9 percent in Indiana) reported no vacant buildings, the number of vacant retail spaces did not appear excessive, at least in the larger towns. Smaller towns generally had higher vacancy rates. (For more detailed discussion see Ayres 1990; Stone 1989; and Leistritz et al. 1989).

The average number of stores of different types for different size towns is important in helping business leaders assess their situation. Table 5 (p. 13) shows this information for the surveyed towns, as reported by the city clerks. The numbers vary among the different size towns, but the top five stores among all towns in each state generally were restaurants, gasoline stations, grocery stores, hardware stores and taverns/liquor stores. A more detailed list, taken from the Iowa Department of Revenue sales tax permit computer tapes, is shown in Appendix Table 5 (p. 32). Stone (1989) reports that, when the *official* state figures were compared to those reported by the city clerks, the number of stores reported by the clerks generally matched the state figures quite closely; however, in several cases, the numbers reported by the clerks were slightly lower than those reported by the state.

Another statistic that can help a town's businesspeople determine the appropriate business mix is the average number of persons per store. These numbers can be derived by merely dividing the state population by the total number of stores in a category reported by the state. Appendix Table 6 (p. 34) shows the results for Iowa for most three-digit SIC code stores. The stores are arrayed from the fewest persons per store to the most. By comparing a town's trade area population to these numbers, one can get a good idea of the threshold of store types.

Findings of Community Interviews

Thirty-seven communities were selected for in-depth case studies: 12 in Indiana, 12 in Iowa and 13 in North Dakota (see Figures 1-3, pp. 4-6, and Appendix Tables 2-4, pp. 27-31). These towns range in population from about 600 to 5,000 and appear to be representative of the states' small- and moderate-sized trade centers. In all three states, the communities were quite diverse. In Indiana, all of the communities were located on a federal highway and all but one community was within 30 miles of an urban area of 50,000 or more population. In contrast, one community in North Dakota was 113 miles from a city of more than 10,000 population and 25 miles from a federal highway. Communities highly dependent upon the energy industry and considered "atypical" were not included in the North Dakota sample.

The communities were geographically distributed across each of the states and represented a variety of economic bases. Communities in Indiana were more dependent on goods-producing industries as a source of employment and income, while Iowa and North Dakota communities were more dependent on agriculture. Fifteen of the 37 communities were county seat towns and derived some benefit from this additional traffic. Some of the communities had special tourist attractions such as "the Grotto," a religious shrine in West Bend, Iowa, and "Amish Acres," an educational Amish farm in Nappanee, Indiana.

Table 1. Number of Respondents, Percent of Cities Having an Active Organization Concerned with Retail Trade, and Activities of Those Organizations, by City Size Group, Indiana, Iowa and North Dakota, 1988

Item	Population Size Group		
	2,500 - 5,000	1,000 - 2,499	500 - 999
Number responding:			
Indiana	40	86	95
Iowa	45	122	161
North Dakota	4	44	40
Percent of group having an organization:			
Indiana	70.3	58.8	41.8
Iowa	93.5	85.5	55.6
North Dakota	100.0	93.2	75.0
Percent of group indicating specific organization activities:			
Promote/maintain business			
Indiana	66.7	84.6	54.2
Iowa	71.1	69.7	50.3
North Dakota	75.0	54.5	37.5
Re-open/attract new business			
Indiana	36.4	38.5	66.7
Iowa	51.1	40.2	62.7
North Dakota	50.0	40.9	60.9
Commercial services/social activities			
Indiana	54.5	23.1	41.7
Iowa	40.0	37.7	39.8
North Dakota	0.0	40.9	25.0
Tourist promotion			
Indiana	51.5	23.1	29.2
Iowa	55.6	19.7	24.8
North Dakota	50.0	6.8	0.0

The key findings of the community interviews are summarized in the sections that follow. These findings are grouped into five major categories: (1) organizational techniques, (2) business financing, (3) business recruitment, (4) promotional campaigns and (5) critical needs of business communities.

Organizational Techniques

The more successful towns generally appeared to have stronger community organizations and better local cooperation. The smaller towns usually had a business group without any paid employees. Most of these groups had officers and/or a board of directors. The larger towns and a few of the intermediate size towns had Chambers of Commerce. A strong Chamber of Commerce was often the point of community promotion activities. Twelve of the 37 communities hired a part-time or

Table 2. Opinions of "How City's Retail Sector is Doing," by City Population Size Group, Indiana, Iowa and North Dakota, 1988

	Population Size Group			
Item	2,500 - 5,000	1,000 - 2,499	500 - 999	% of Total
	------------- *percent of population group* -------------			
Indiana				
Done fairly well	38.5	20.2	13.0	20.5
Held its own	35.9	38.1	37.0	37.2
Declined somewhat	20.5	35.7	30.4	30.7
Gone down the tubes	5.1	6.0	19.6	11.6
Iowa				
Done fairly well	26.7	13.1	11.2	14.0
Held its own	42.2	36.1	37.9	37.9
Declined somewhat	31.1	45.1	36.0	38.7
Gone down the tubes	0.0	5.7	14.9	9.5
North Dakota				
Done fairly well	75.0	43.2	47.5	46.6
Held its own	25.0	43.1	32.5	37.5
Declined somewhat	0.0	9.1	15.0	11.4
Gone down the tubes	0.0	4.5	5.0	4.5

full-time person to coordinate Chamber and economic development activities. The presence of a Chamber executive or development coordinator seemed to be a key factor contributing to the community's success. The employment of a development coordinator appeared to be a definite trend among the larger towns. Several comments indicated that such people were instrumental in bringing the business community together, developing promotions, and in recruiting needed businesses to town.

Lisbon, North Dakota, appeared to have one of the best organized development efforts. Their economic development effort is organized as an integral component of the Chamber of Commerce. An organizational chart illustrating the relationship of the various committees is shown in Figure 4 (p. 35) in the Appendix.

Several communities offered examples of cooperation between county and city governments. The county and city may combine their resources to hire a full-time development coordinator. One county and city in North Dakota had joined with two other counties and several other cities to fund a tri-county development office. Although such cooperation is ideal, especially in more remote rural areas, there is concern that the larger, more dominant towns will receive the most benefits and that the smaller towns will lose out. County officials were sometimes reluctant to help fund such development efforts because of possible inequities.

Table 3. Types of Stores That Had Done "Best" by Town Size Group, Indiana, Iowa and North Dakota, 1988

| | Population Size Group | | | |
State/Store Type	2,500 - 5,000	1,000 - 2,499	500 - 999	Total
	----- *percent of group indicating "best" store type[1]* -----			
Indiana				
Grocery store	72.5	67.4	61.1	65.6
Restaurant/fast food	70.0	39.5	49.5	49.3
Gasoline/service station	12.5	12.8	23.2	17.2
Hardware	10.0	17.4	13.7	14.5
Convenience stores	5.0	12.8	13.7	11.8
Iowa				
Grocery store	24.4	18.4	18.0	19.1
Restaurant/fast food	18.3	14.1	16.1	15.6
Convenience stores	4.4	10.6	12.4	10.4
Farm supply	0.0	4.4	10.5	6.3
Hardware	7.0	6.3	3.4	5.2
North Dakota				
Grocery store	25.0	79.6	50.0	63.6
Restaurant/fast food	75.0	31.8	32.5	34.1
Gasoline/service station	25.0	18.2	25.0	21.6
Farm equipment/auto	25.0	20.5	17.5	17.0
Hardware	25.0	15.6	2.5	15.9

[1] Some respondents named more than one store type as having done "best."

In the "successful" communities interviewed, the organizations worked together in a spirit of cooperation and strong commitment. For example, in Sunman, Indiana, 95 percent of the businesses belonged to and were actively involved with the Chamber of Commerce. There appeared to be strong ties between city and county government, the Chamber of Commerce, and other community groups such as the Jaycees and Kiwanis.

Business Financing

The availability of adequate financing is often seen as the key to rural economic development (Daniels and Crockett 1988). However, most of the *successful* business-people surveyed indicated that financing the business was little or no problem. In most of the communities in the three states, local banks were still regarded as a reliable source of operating capital for *established* businesses. It was for new or aspiring businesspeople that capital restrictions were found to be a problem. Local bankers indicated that a new business would need a sound business plan and substantial owner equity to qualify for a loan.

11

Table 4. Types of Stores That Had Not Done Well, by Town Size Group, Indiana, Iowa and North Dakota, 1988

State/Store Type	Population Size Group			
	2,500 - 5,000	1,000 - 2,499	500 - 999	Total
	----------------------------- percent[2] -----------------------------			
Indiana				
Restaurant/fast food	12.5	27.9	15.8	19.9
Clothing	35.0	14.0	6.3	14.5
Hardware	10.0	12.8	11.6	11.8
Grocery store	5.0	10.5	8.4	8.6
Gasoline/service station	7.5	5.8	10.5	8.1
Iowa				
Restaurants/fast food	1.6	14.6	12.2	12.0
Clothing	29.5	10.5	5.4	10.6
Grocery store	6.6	8.7	13.6	10.6
Hardware	6.6	10.1	12.2	10.6
Convenience stores	8.2	6.9	4.5	6.0
North Dakota				
Farm equipment/auto	25.0	27.2	30.0	25.0
Clothing	25.0	22.7	20.0	21.6
Tavern/liquor store	0.0	15.9	12.5	13.6
Building/lumber	0.0	15.9	12.1	13.6
Hardware	0.0	18.2	5.0	11.4

[2] Some respondents named more than one type of store as not having done well.

Respondents from the financial institutions indicated that most of the new or aspiring businesspeople were undercapitalized, and many had little or no experience in running a business. Most bankers viewed loans to undercapitalized, inexperienced businesspeople as risky and imprudent. Some bankers indicated that they sometimes made these types of loans when Small Business Administration loan guarantees could be secured. SBA, however, has also had a substantial number of foreclosures in the recent past, and they too require a significant down payment (20 to 35 percent) from the borrower. Thus, it appears that entrepreneurship in many rural communities may be constrained by the limited number of people who have sufficient personal wealth to finance a new firm.

Several respondents indicated that their towns had sought state or federal grants or other financial help on behalf of businesses in the community. However, at the federal level, grant programs have been severely reduced. At the state level, grants are being given very judiciously because of the inability to resolve problems of equity connected with such programs.

A recent development that may exacerbate the problems of financing rural businesses is the growth of branch banking. The managers of branch banks were seen

Table 5. Average Number of Stores by Type and City Size Group, as Reported by Town Clerks, Indiana, Iowa and North Dakota, 1988

	Population Size Group			
State/Store Type	2,500 - 5,000	1,000 - 2,499	500 - 999	Total
Indiana				
Restaurant/fast food	6.0	3.0	1.9	3.0
Gasoline/service station	3.8	2.4	1.4	2.2
Tavern/liquor store	3.6	2.3	1.5	2.2
Grocery store	1.8	1.4	1.0	1.3
Convenience stores	1.7	1.1	0.7	1.1
Automobile dealer	2.5	1.2	0.4	1.1
Iowa				
Restaurant/fast food	6.1	2.8	1.5	2.6
Tavern/liquor store	3.6	2.4	1.6	2.2
Gasoline/service station	3.7	2.3	1.6	2.2
Convenience stores	0.9	1.5	2.7	2.0
Grocery store	1.8	1.2	0.8	1.1
Automobile dealer	2.5	1.0	0.5	1.0
North Dakota				
Tavern/liquor store	5.3	4.5	2.3	3.5
Restaurant/fast food	7.3	3.4	1.9	2.9
Gasoline/service station	3.3	3.5	2.0	2.8
Grocery store	2.8	2.0	1.2	1.7
Farm equipment/auto	2.8	2.0	0.8	1.5
Hardware	2.3	1.7	0.6	1.2

---

as having less community interest and concern than the typical proprietor of a locally-owned establishment. Branch bank managers were perceived as preferring to invest deposits in larger, more stable communities, but some local branch managers may have only limited decision-making authority. Credit unions appeared to be filling some of the gap created by the restructuring of the banking industry, and they appeared to be more willing to make loans to businesses in smaller towns.

The most critical capital shortage for new or expanding firms was equity financing and long-term debt. To overcome this problem some entrepreneurs developed creative solutions. For example, a prospective restaurant operator in North Dakota raised much of his capital in the form of small personal notes with 10 to 15 years duration. Another person in North Dakota, seeking to establish a farm machinery dealership, was able to obtain financing only after an established businessman agreed to co-sign the note. In Iowa, limited partnerships were used in some communities to provide capital for an entrepreneur with the ability, but without the capital. "Silent partners" provide a share of the capital in return for a pro-rata share of the returns. A few communities had established a revolving loan fund ear-marked for new businesses.

Transferring the ownership of an existing business can be almost as difficult as financing a new one. This study revealed several instances of seemingly viable businesses in the communities that were likely to close because no new proprietor could be found. In Iowa, there were several cases of old-line businesses that were sold through owner financing. This method of buying "on contract" can be very beneficial to both the seller and buyer. However, in situations where the seller is selling a "run down" store and the buyer is too inexperienced to realize it, the result can be disastrous. Another suggestion offered by the community and business leaders was to develop an "opportunity network" to bring sellers in contact with potential buyers.

Business Recruitment

Business recruitment efforts by these communities included efforts to not only attract new basic sector employers, but also to round out the local retail sector. Frequently, the retail recruitment efforts were aimed at replacing a business that had been lost previously. In North Dakota, for example, certain towns were recruiting automobile dealers, farm machinery dealers and furniture stores. Indiana communities targeted clothing and discount stores, medical services and pharmacies.

Local development organizations often emphasize that their efforts are aimed at attracting noncompeting stores, but the study results cast some doubt on the wisdom of this approach. On numerous occasions in several communities, the study team was told that the loss of one auto dealer, machinery dealer, etc. hurts the remaining one(s). The desire of consumers to comparison shop was the reason most frequently cited to explain this situation.

Nearly all of the surveyed towns in the three states indicated some effort aimed toward recruiting new business and industry. In most towns the major effort was aimed at attracting industry from another location, although some towns had benefitted from expanded existing businesses. However, industry and jobs do not guarantee the success of the retail sector. There are many examples in the three states where towns have strong industrial sectors, but the retail sector is so weak that most of the money earned in town is spent elsewhere. This situation negates one of the supposed benefits of having industry—the multiplier effect.

The multiplier effect is based on the concept that money earned in a community will in large measure be spent locally for goods and services, and that the entities that supply those goods and services will in turn spend a substantial part of their increased receipts within the local economy. When a community's economy is quite diverse and self-sufficient, the multiplier effect could cause the original economic activity (e.g., new plant expenditures) to be doubled or even more (Gordon and Mulkey 1978; Leistritz, Murdock and Leholm 1982). But when wage earners in a town spend their money elsewhere, the multiplier effect does not occur and this benefit is lost.

Promotional Campaigns

Nearly every town in all three states had some type of promotional campaign to encourage shopping in the community. Farmer appreciation days were typical in the smaller towns in Iowa and North Dakota. It was not always clear, however, that these promotions were particularly effective in boosting retail sales. In North Dakota, "hometown dollars" were typical. These were interest free loans to residents from a local bank with businesses absorbing a small interest charge for funds spent in their store. These promotions were typically run during the pre-Christmas period.

Some towns sponsored local events that combined a fun time with shopping promotions. Examples of these are Jesse James Days in Adair, Iowa; Fourth of July celebrations; Valentine's Day—Night on the Town; Hog Wild Days; Window Walk; Woodburn Days in Woodburn, Indiana; Apple Festival; Art Festival; and Haubstadt, Indiana's, Sommerfest.

Several towns had annual events that attracted national audiences, such as Dyersville, Iowa, with its National Farm Toy Show and Ida Grove, Iowa, with its Aviation Expo. Still other towns capitalized on local attractions. For example, West Bend, Iowa, attracted visitors from afar with its Grotto; and Adair, Iowa, had some success in attracting visitors to the site of Jesse James' first train robbery. Nappanee, Indiana, drew many visitors to the surrounding Amish community and Amish Acres, a working Amish farm.

Some communities took advantage of the town's location. For example, local leaders in Carrington, North Dakota, have been promoting the town as a natural site for meetings and conventions because it is located almost equal distance from the state's four major population centers. Two communities in Indiana attempted to capture visitors to the nearby state park.

In the three states, it was found that certain services can be a major attraction. A medical services complex in particular was frequently cited as a factor that drew people to some towns from a wide area. The quality of medical facilities was also a factor influencing the residential decisions of retiring farm families. In North Dakota, schools and grain elevators were frequently cited as attractions. Tipton, Indiana, took advantage of visitors who came to the 4-H Center to attend antique shows, auctions and other regional-wide events.

An example of coordinated promotion that was common to most of the communities was a monthly or bi-weekly advertising pamphlet with information from a number of local businesses. A variation on this theme was found in Hettinger, North Dakota, where advertising materials from a number of businesses were distributed monthly in a plastic mailbag.

When asked to evaluate the effectiveness of local media for advertising and community promotion, most respondents indicated that a home-owned newspaper could be a major asset to a community. When the local paper was owned by a syndicate, residents often complained that not enough attention was given to local events. Three communities in Indiana developed their own newsletter-type newspaper in the absence of a community newspaper. Local radio stations also received favorable reviews in several of the towns. Few of the businesses visited used television advertising extensively, but several towns were experimenting with television ads to promote the community in general.

Several of Indiana's businesspeople commented that the most effective promotion was word-of-mouth. The merchants believed the customers knew them, and they knew the customers. It was therefore important to provide outstanding service. Their reputation was very important, and it was the major reason old customers kept coming back and new customers came in.

Several Indiana communities promoted the entire community for industrial and business development and participated in "Hoosier Hospitality Days," a state-sponsored event to promote Indiana communities to industrial prospects. Brochures, displays, videotapes, billboards and other materials were developed to promote the entire community.

Critical Needs of Business Communities

The ultimate objective of the community interviews was to identify major needs common to the business communities of small rural towns. The interviews revealed some needs that could be addressed only through a communitywide effort, and others that reflected specific problems common to many local businesses.

The most basic among the problems requiring communitywide action is the need for economic diversification. Many of the communities, especially in North Dakota, have been heavily dependent on agriculture. Others, such as in Indiana, have been dependent upon one or two major manufacturing firms. In either case, the need is to broaden the community's economic base so that it is not so dependent, and susceptible to fluctuations, on any one sector.

Some of the communities studied had achieved at least limited success in broadening their economic base. Their experience indicates that successful economic development efforts require a long-term commitment and effective coordination of effort among the community's business and civic leaders, as well as an awareness of resources that may be available from higher levels of government. The presence of a paid development coordinator or Chamber executive seemed to be a critical factor in assuring continuity of community efforts. However, smaller towns may not be able to afford the services of such an individual. A county- or regionwide economic development office may be a partial solution in such cases.

Examination of the communities that have succeeded in broadening their economic base also suggests that both recruitment and entrepreneurship have played important roles in their success. Perhaps most important is the need for communities to take a strategic approach to planning and implementing their economic development efforts. Such an approach emphasizes (1) determining community goals and (2) identifying available resources and constraints with the aim of (3) identifying the town's comparative advantages relative to other towns and localities. These advantages, which could be based on a variety of factors including the natural resource base, location, the skills of the labor force, or the availability of serviced land, can serve as a basis for identifying development and promotion opportunities (Henshall Hansen Associates 1988).

The businesspeople and community leaders interviewed indicated the importance of other communitywide issues on retail business success. One critical factor was the importance of the location and hours of the local bank. In one Indiana community, the local bank closed its downtown office and opened a new office on the fringe of town. This hurt the downtown businesses and prompted the development of other new businesses at the edge of town. Another community had strict zoning ordinances that prohibited this fringe development. The hours of the bank were also deemed important. As one merchant claimed, "People shop where they can cash their checks." When the bank closes at 3 p.m. or is closed on Saturday, retail losses result.

Highways, sanitary sewer systems, schools and medical facilities are also critical issues in rural retail business success. Highways bring people to and through the community, but congested highways pose a safety problem. By-passes to divert traffic from the downtown may alleviate traffic congestion, but encourage fringe development. This was a major issue in some of the communities.

The up-dating, expansion or installation of a sanitary sewer system was another important issue in several of the communities studied. Sunman, Indiana, was under a court order to install a sewer system, but the $1 million cost posed a major problem. Several residents believed this issue thwarted their attempts to attract new businesses to the community.

The location of the school was also a major concern in many of the communities. Some leaders were lamenting the loss of the school in the 1960s, others were facing a current loss of the school, while still others believed that the nearby regional school was a major asset. In all cases, the school was considered to be a significant factor in drawing customers to the community.

Medical facilities were viewed in the same manner. If the community did not have a doctor, the leaders were active in recruiting a doctor. They felt the absence of medical services provided one more reason for customers to go outside the community to shop.

The businesspeople in the towns surveyed identified several critical needs. Foremost among these was to stem the outshopping (i.e., keeping customers in town to shop). In some of the communities, many residents work outside of the community and therefore shop out of town. Even in communities where the residents work there, larger urban areas offer many attractions to the rural consumers. Many of the merchants interviewed recognize this fact but feel that their competitive advantage is outstanding, "going-out-of-the way" service. And that's what many of the merchants were trying to provide.

Many of the successful merchants were older people who had operated the store for many years and had made no provisions for transferring the business to someone else. If the business cannot be sold, the business closes and is frequently gone forever. There is a need for town leaders to anticipate when such a situation is arising and to find ways to transfer operation of the business to a capable person before the business closes. Although this was a problem identified in the towns, they had not dealt well with the problem.

Both business proprietors and community leaders indicated a high level of interest in technical assistance for businesses. Areas frequently mentioned as deserving more attention included: financial management, developing business plans, merchandising, inventory management, personnel management, and customer relations. Although these needs were expressed, few of the people surveyed had taken advantage of such courses offered through universities, the Extension Service, Small Business Development Centers, or other available sources.

A critical need mentioned by several respondents was the ability to attract and retrain quality personnel. It appeared that, like customers, many good employees gravitated to larger towns to seek better employment. The need was indicated for information on personnel management, employee stock ownership plans, and other aspects of employee relations.

Finally, the most pervasive problem mentioned was difficulty in obtaining equity or long-term debt financing for new ventures or major expansions. While some of the reported reluctance by local lenders to supply funds to new or expanding enterprises may be a rational response to adverse local economic conditions, our observations suggest that rural entrepreneurs generally have less access to various forms of equity capital than those located in more urbanized areas. State or local initiatives (e.g., revolving loan funds, cooperative financing or limited partnerships) to make venture capital more readily available to businesses in rural areas could potentially help resolve this problem, although careful analysis of potential investments would certainly be required. In addition, improved access to technical assistance in developing a business plan and making key financial management decisions could aid some potential entrepreneurs in gaining approval of their loans.

Findings of the Retail Trade Survey

The following results were gathered from personal interviews with some of the better retailers in 12 towns in Indiana and 12 towns in Iowa. North Dakota used a structured questionnaire of business establishments in 12 towns. (Personal interviews were also conducted with key businesses in the 13th North Dakota town, Lisbon, but the findings are not included in this tabulation. This was because Lisbon served as the pretest for the North Dakota business questionnaire, which was then revised substantially.)

Information about the number of responding businesses in each town in each state is summarized in Table 6 (p. 19).

18

Table 6. Number of Questionnaires Completed by Businesses in Indiana, Iowa and North Dakota

| Population/Town | Number of Businesses Completing Questionnaire | | | | | |
	Indiana		Iowa		North Dakota	
500 - 999 Population	Sunman	4	Adair	3	Gwinner	10
	Gosport	2	Ireton	3	Maddock	13
	Trafalgar	4	West Bend	4	New England	12
	Darlington	3			Pembina	6
					Stanton	5
1,000 - 2,499 Population	Oxford	6	Allison	3	Ashley	23
	Westport	4	Bancroft	6	Crosby	31
	Haubstadt	5	Guthrie Center	3	Hettinger	37
	Woodburn	3	Ida Grove	4	Stanley	32
			Manson	5		
			St. Ansgar	3		
2,500 - 5,000 Population	Tipton	6	Dyersville	5	Bottineau	42
	Nappanee	3	Manchester	3	Carrington	42
	Spencer	4	Sheldon	3	Rugby	44
	Loogootee	2				
TOTAL		46		45		297

Various characteristics of the surveyed businesses are summarized in Appendix Table 7 (p. 36). Business types encountered most frequently were restaurants, grocery stores, farm equipment dealers, hardware stores, farm supply centers and clothing stores in North Dakota; hardware stores, grocery stores, department stores, farm implement stores and automobile dealers in Iowa; and hardware stores, drugstores, flower/gift shops and grocery stores in Indiana. A greater number of farm related businesses were found in Iowa and North Dakota than were found in Indiana.

The majority of businesses surveyed were locally owned (82 percent in Iowa, 97 percent in North Dakota and 87 percent in Indiana). The firms had typically been in existence about 30 years (mean), but under the present ownership for less than 10 years (median).

The typical business reported that its trade area had a radius of about 40 miles in North Dakota, 28 miles in Indiana and 26 miles in Iowa. Good service was most often cited as the competitive advantage of businesses in all three states.

Not surprisingly, almost all of the retailers viewed customer relations as "very important" to their business (see Appendix Table 8, p. 38). However, when asked in North Dakota how frequently business owners or their employees attended training sessions or courses on customer relations, almost 43 percent replied "never" and another 10 percent indicated that such training occurred less than once per year. (This question was not asked in Indiana or Iowa.) Seventy percent of surveyed businesses in Indiana and North Dakota, and 91 percent of surveyed businesses in Iowa believed that price markdowns were important in their business. About 40 percent in North Dakota, 39 percent in Indiana and 16 percent in Iowa have markdowns continuously. The majority of businesses rated their store displays as good or very good.

The average business spent about 2.5 percent of their annual sales volume on advertising. Newspaper was the most heavily used advertising media, accounting for nearly one-half of advertising expenditures (see Appendix Table 9, p. 39).

Businesses surveyed in North Dakota employed an average of 3.8 full-time workers, in Iowa 7, and in Indiana 6. North Dakota firms employed an average of 2.6 year-round, part-time employees; Iowa firms 4.1; and Indiana firms 3.7. Few hired part-time seasonal help (see Appendix Table 10, p. 40).

The mean age of the business proprietor or manager was about 44 years old in North Dakota, 46 years old in Iowa, and 42 years old in Indiana. The average educational level of the business owner was one to two years beyond high school. Only a few had college degrees (see Appendix Table 11, p. 41). The business owners' involvement in the local Chamber or business club differed somewhat among the states. Nearly three-fourths were active in North Dakota, 89 percent were active in Iowa, and 54 percent were active in Indiana. Almost all businesses banked locally.

Business operators were asked what change had occurred in their sales volume during the last two years and what change they anticipated over the next two years (see Appendix Table 12, p. 42). The average operator reported that volume had increased, and they expected this to continue to increase in the next two years.

In evaluating the success of their business, opinions varied across the states. In Iowa, 64 percent responded "very successful," compared to 54 percent in Indiana and 43 percent in North Dakota. A larger number of the businesspeople were satisfied with the success of their business and the associated lifestyle it supports (67 percent in Iowa, 72 percent in Indiana, and 60 percent in North Dakota).

Summary and Conclusions

Three general observations emerged in this three-state study. One was the constant change that is occurring in small rural communities. While such communities may appear stable, the study found a great deal of turn-over and change. From the time the initial mail questionnaire was sent to the communities until the in-depth interviews were conducted (a period of four to six months), some retail businesses closed while new businesses opened. Rural communities are dynamic. One of the struggles for local leaders is the ability to deal with this constant change.

A second observation was that there is no "ideal" community. While better-than-average retail communities were chosen for this study, they still confronted many problems. Some communities had a relatively strong retail sector yet were struggling to diversify the economic base or were threatened with the loss of their elementary school. Even within the retail sector, while some businesses were doing well, others were near the point of closing their doors. Some communities had an active business organization, but did not have available financing for new businesses. There were no communities that exhibited outstanding efforts in all arenas of the community. Most were struggling to do the best they could with available resources. This reality of small town life reflects the constant change in the community, the dependency on volunteer leadership to deal with the change, and the limited availability of human and financial resources to assist in community efforts.

The third general finding that emerged was the similarity of the issues. The researchers were expecting to find different issues regarding the retail community due to the differences in economic base and degree of urbanization in the three states. However, the concerns and issues expressed in the communities were nearly identical.

A number of critical needs were identified in the study that have implications for community development practitioners, researchers and policymakers. These include:

The importance of a strong economic base. Most of the communities in the three states were attempting to diversify and strengthen their economic base. The communities that were successful in attracting new businesses had a long-term commitment to the effort and had established an effective coordinated effort among the community's business and civic leaders. The leaders of these communities were also aware of available outside resources and had pursued them. The presence of a paid development coordinator or Chamber executive seemed to be a critical factor in assuring continuity of community efforts. However, smaller towns may not be able to afford the services of such an individual. A county- or region-wide economic development office may be a partial solution in such cases.

This study found that most communities pursue only a limited range of opportunities to diversify the economic base. The primary strategy is trying to attract a major industry. While this approach may prove successful in a few places, it is not the best option in most rural communities. Research is needed on the costs and benefits of various economic development strategies in various types of communities.

Research is also needed on whether placing limited resources in a part-time or full-time economic development person is the best use of resources. The study found that this was a popular trend among the larger communities. However, if the community had not undertaken some sort of planning process or had hired an inexperienced person, efforts could be futile and leave the community quite frustrated. Research is needed regarding the conditions under which hiring such a person works best.

A third area of needed research is in the area of intergovernmental agreements for multicommunity efforts. The study found this to be an alternative that communities were considering. Information is needed regarding how multicommunity liaisons are developed and the costs and benefits of this approach.

The need for business management training. A second lesson learned was the importance of technical assistance for rural businesses. Both business proprietors and community leaders indicated a high level of interest in technical assistance. Areas frequently mentioned included: financial management, developing business plans, merchandising, inventory management, personnel management and customer relations. Many of these topics are currently offered as extension programs through colleges and universities. The researchers found a general lack of knowledge about available programs. It was also learned that many of the businesses that are part of a national chain have access to technical information, while the locally owned stores do not have such assistance available. Assistance is needed to help identify the particular training needs in the community and the nearest available source for such training.

The need for mechanisms to transfer business operations. Many of the successful small-town merchants are older people who have operated a store that has been in the family for a long time. The study found that when these people approach retirement age, most have not made provisions for transferring the business to someone else. Consequently, the business is closed and gone forever.

Assistance is needed to develop creative mechanisms to transfer the operation of the business to capable new owners before the business closes. Researchers can play a critical role in examining ways in which such transfers can take place and under what conditions.

The need for innovative financing mechanisms for new or aspiring businesses. This study found a pervasive problem in obtaining equity or long-term debt financing for new ventures. Local lenders are reluctant to supply funds to new enterprises that are perceived as high risk loans. Improved access to technical assistance in developing a business plan and making key financial management decisions could aid some potential entrepreneurs in gaining approval of their loans.

The importance of planning for the future. Perhaps the most important single lesson from the study is the need for both individual businesses and communities to adopt a strategic approach in planning their future. This approach features an outlook that anticipates the future, reflecting a readiness to make the most of opportunities arising from change as well as acting to forestall potential threats.

References

Ayres, Janet S. 1990. *A Study of Successful Retail Communities in Indiana.* West Lafayette, IN: Purdue University, Department of Agricultural Economics.

Daniels, Belden H. and Catherine A. Crockett. 1988. *Rural North Carolina Development Finance Action Plan.* Boston, MA: Counsel for Community Development Inc.

Ekstrom, Brenda L. and F. Larry Leistritz. 1988. *Rural Community Decline and Revitalization: An Annotated Bibliography.* New York: Garland Publishing Inc.

Gordon, John and David Mulkey. 1978. "Income Multipliers for Community Impact Analysis—What Size Is Reasonable?" *Journal of the Community Development Society* 9(2):85-93.

Henshall Hansen Associates. 1988. *Small Towns Study in Victoria*. Fitzroy, Victoria, Australia: Victoria Department of Agriculture and Rural Affairs.

John, DeWitt, Sandra S. Batie and Kim Norris. 1988. *A Brighter Future for Rural America? Strategies for Communities and States*. Washington, D.C.: National Governors' Association.

Johnson, Bruce and Joel Young. 1987. *Trends in Retail Sales Activity Across Nebraska's Counties and Communities*. Lincoln, NE: University of Nebraska, Department of Agricultural Economics.

Leistritz, F. Larry, Janet Wanzek and Rita R. Hamm. 1990. *North Dakota 1990: Patterns and Trends in Economic Activity and Population*. Agricultural Economics Statistical Series Report No. 46. Fargo, ND: North Dakota State University, Department of Agricultural Economics.

Leistritz, F. Larry, Timothy L. Mortensen, Holly Bastow-Shoop, Joan Braaten-Grabanski, Alan Schuler and Julie Fedorenko. 1989. *Revitalizing the Retail Trade Sector in Rural Communities: Experiences of 13 North Dakota Towns*. Agricultural Economics Report No. 250. Fargo, ND: North Dakota State University, Department of Agricultural Economics.

Leistritz, F. Larry, Steve H. Murdock and Arlen G. Leholm. 1982. "Local Economic Changes Associated With Rapid Growth." *Coping With Rapid Growth in Rural Communities* 25-66. Edited by B. Weber and R. Howell. Boulder, CO: Westview Press.

Stone, Kenneth E. 1989. *A Study of Small Iowa Towns With Successful Retail Sectors*. Ames, IA: Iowa State University, Department of Economics.

Stone, Kenneth E. 1988. *A Guide to Using Sales Tax Data to Assess Business Risks in Community Development Extension Programs*. Ames, IA: Iowa State University, Department of Economics.

Stone, Kenneth E. and James M. McConnon Jr. 1980. *Retail Sales Migration in the Midwestern United States*. Ames, IA: Iowa State University, Department of Economics.

Appendix Tables

Appendix Table 1. Deflated Taxable Sales by Population Size Group, Iowa, 1980-1988

| Town Population | Deflated Taxable Sales (1988 $) | | Percentage Change |
	1980	1988	1980 - 1988
Over 50,000	$ 6,653,100,000	$ 6,996,100,000	5.2
25,000-50,000	2,327,500,000	2,004,900,000	-13.9
10,000-25,000	1,405,900,000	1,372,500,000	-2.4
5,000-10,000	2,332,200,000	2,048,400,000	-12.2
2,500-5,000	1,629,900,000	1,211,000,000	-25.7
1,000-2,500	1,685,700,000	1,131,800,000	-32.9
500-1,000	962,100,000	462,500,000	-51.9
Less than 500	566,200,000	291,700,000	-48.9
Rural	1,107,800,000	625,400,000	-43.5
Other	75,100,000	31,400,000	-58.2
State Total	$18,745,500,000	$16,175,700,000	-13.7

Source: Stone (1989)

Appendix Table 2. Profile of Indiana Cities Selected for In-depth Interviews

Town	Population (1980)	Distance From Federal Highway (miles)	Distance From City Over 10,000 (miles)
500 - 999 Population			
Sunman	955	3	25
Gosport	788	4	13
Trafalgar		9	6
Darlington	875	3	7
1,000 - 2,499 Population			
Oxford	1,255	16	16
Westport	1,439	15	15
Haubstadt	1,407	1	13
Woodburn	1,039	2	15
2,500 - 5,000 Population			
Tipton	4,794	5	15
Nappanee	4,561	0	15
Spencer	2,647	0	15
Loogootee	3,143	0	14

27

Appendix Table 3. Profile of Iowa Cities Selected for In-depth Interviews

City	Pull Factor 1980	Pull Factor 1988	Change 80 to 88	Population 1980	Population 1986	Change 80 to 86	Nominal Taxable Sales 1980	Nominal Taxable Sales 1988	Change 80 to 88
			(%)			(%)	---- $000 ----		(%)
500 - 999 Population Group									
Adair	2.32	1.44	-37.9	883	840	-4.9	10,066	7,886	-21.7
Ireton	2.08	1.52	-26.9	588	570	-3.1	6,420	5,669	-11.7
West Bend	1.55	1.34	-13.5	941	900	-4.4	7,506	7,877	4.9
1,000 - 2,499 Population Group									
Allison	2.17	1.97	-9.2	1,132	980	-13.4	12,966	12,628	-2.6
Bancroft	1.80	1.11	-38.3	1,082	940	-13.1	10,154	6,786	-33.2
Guthrie Center	1.74	1.56	-10.3	1,713	1,610	-6.1	15,676	20,296	29.5
Ida Grove	2.27	2.23	-1.8	2,285	2,360	3.3	27,220	34,402	26.4
Manson	1.60	3.37	110.6	1,924	1,680	-12.7	16,251	36,917	127.2
St. Ansgar	1.06	2.01	89.6	1,100	1,050	-4.5	6,085	13,806	126.9
2,500 - 5,000 Population Group									
Dyersville	1.94	1.48	-23.7	3,825	3,940	3.1	38,930	37,967	-2.5
Manchester	1.94	1.61	-17.1	4,942	4,860	-1.7	50,362	51,032	1.3
Sheldon	1.57	1.85	17.8	5,003	4,710	-5.9	41,306	56,833	37.6

Deflated Taxable Sales			Net Stores Open/ Close	Number of Core Stores	Distance From Federal Highway	Distance From City Over 10,000	Total Tax Permit Holders
1980	1988	Change 80 to 88					
---- $000 ----		(%)	+/-	(No.)	(Miles)	(Miles)	(No.)
14,392	7,886	-45.2	-8	17	0	52	49
9,179	5,669	-38.2	2	8	7	57	41
10,732	7,877	-26.6	4	16	10	58	52
18,538	12,628	-31.9	-16	16	16	32	61
14,518	6,786	-53.3	5	18	0	46	54
22,413	20,296	-9.4	-34	22	11	50	97
38,918	34,402	-11.6	15	30	0	53	142
23,235	36,917	58.9	-5	18	8	18	84
8,700	13,806	58.7	-4	13	0	35	58
55,661	37,967	-31.8	12	38	1	25	162
72,006	51,032	-29.1	-2	52	1	45	220
59,058	56,833	-3.8	10	48	0	35	243

Appendix Table 4. Profile of North Dakota Cities Selected for In-depth Interviews

City	Pull Factor			Population			Nominal Taxable Sales		
	1980	1987	Change 80 to 87	1980	1986	Change 80 to 86	1980	1987	Change 80 to 87
			(%)			(%)	---- $000 ----		(%)
500 - 999 Population Group									
Gwinner	1.51	1.97	29.90	725	676	-6.8	4,948	7,530	52.2
Maddock	0.85	0.39	-54.50	677	598	-11.7	5,066	2,548	-49.7
New England	0.84	0.33	-61.20	825	724	-12.2	5,589	2,280	-59.2
Pembina	0.18	0.23	27.50	673	677	0.6	1,270	1,916	50.9
Stanton	na	na	na	623	729	17.0	494	559	13.1
1,000 - 2,499 Population Group									
Ashley	0.49	0.53	9.00	1,192	1,125	-5.6	3,919	4,553	16.2
Crosby	0.68	0.33	-51.20	1,469	1,429	-2.7	8,316	6,262	-25.1
Hettinger	0.75	0.86	14.30	1,739	1,794	3.2	10,236	11,771	15
Lisbon	0.77	0.89	16.00	2,283	2,138	-6.4	13,182	17,947	36.1
Stanley	0.63	0.46	-27.80	1,631	1,685	3.3	9,530	8,212	-13.8
2,500 - 5,000 Population Group									
Bottineau	0.88	0.55	-37.80	2,829	2,793	-1.3	23,735	18,868	-20.5
Carrington	0.86	0.74	-14.00	2,641	2,529	-4.2	20,793	18,462	-11.2
Rugby	0.88	0.79	-12.70	3,335	3,086	-7.5	20,166	20,173	0.1

Deflated Taxable Sales			Net Stores Open/ Close	Number of Core Stores[a]	Distance From Federal Highway	Distance From City Over 10,000	Total Tax Permit Holders
1980	1987	Change 80 to 87					
---- $000 ----		(%)	+/-	(No.)	(Miles)	(Miles)	(No.)
6,823	7,530	10.4	0	9	39	84	30
6,986	2,548	-63.5	-6	9	25	113	37
7,707	2,280	-70.4	-2	13	16	26	30
1,751	1,916	9.4	1	8	0	79	21
681	559	-18	-2	5	23	64	16
5,404	4,553	-15.8	-5	20	35	92	50
11,530	6,262	-45.7	-2	22	14	68	71
14,115	11,771	-16.6	1	29	0	68	80
18,178	17,947	-1.3	-5	29	41	71	84
13,142	8,212	-37.5	-7	30	0	54	66
32,731	18,868	-42.4	-1	36	22	76	142
28,674	18,462	-35.6	-7	34	0	42	111
27,809	20,173	-27.5	1	30	0	64	130

[a] Core stores were defined to include grocery stores, convenience stores, restaurants, hardware stores, gas stations, liquor and drug stores, and automobile and farm equipment dealers. These store types were felt to be those most commonly found in, and essential to, small rural business districts.

Appendix Table 5. Average Number of Stores by Type and Population Size Group,[a] Iowa, 1988

| Store Type | Population Size Group | | |
	2,500 - 5,000 n = 115	1,000 - 2,499 n = 320	500 - 999 n = 323
	-------------------- Percent of Population Group --------------------		
Beauty shops	10.40	5.20	2.90
Farm supplies	3.10	2.20	1.50
Drinking places	3.70	2.40	1.60
Eating places	9.40	4.50	1.80
Gasoline stations	5.10	2.80	1.50
General automobile repair	4.00	2.50	1.30
Hobby, toy, craft shops	7.00	3.20	1.40
Used merchandise stores	4.50	2.10	1.00
Grocery stores	2.60	1.40	0.80
Plumbing, heating, A/C service	3.00	1.60	0.85
Farm and garden equipment	2.40	1.10	0.74
Sporting goods stores	3.80	1.50	0.69
Miscellaneous general merchandise	2.20	1.20	0.69
Hardware stores	1.60	1.10	0.53
Direct selling	2.60	1.30	0.56
Lumber and building material	1.70	1.10	0.54
Electricians	1.80	1.10	0.49
Barber shops	2.20	1.30	0.63
General contractors	2.20	1.20	0.49
Carpenters	1.40	0.82	0.42
Reupholstery shops	1.50	0.80	0.33
Auto and home supply	3.10	1.10	0.45
Gift and novelty shops	1.80	0.80	0.33
Radio and TV sales	2.00	0.87	0.29
Paint and wallpaper stores	1.30	0.62	0.25
Automobile dealers	2.30	0.85	0.30
Florists	1.70	0.97	0.28
Radio and TV repair	0.76	0.55	0.22
Car washes	1.20	0.58	0.23

Appendix Table 5. (Continued)

Store Type	Population Size Group		
	2,500 - 5,000 n = 115	1,000 - 2,499 n = 320	500 - 999 n = 323
	------------------ Percent of Population Group ------------------		
Plumbing, heating equipment	1.10	0.38	0.15
Nursery and garden supplies	1.10	0.42	0.15
Furniture stores	1.70	0.55	0.19
Lawn and garden services	0.80	0.43	0.16
Coin-op laundry and cleaners	1.10	0.53	0.18
Hotel/motels	1.60	0.70	0.17
Photo studios	1.60	0.44	0.17
Household appliances	1.10	0.30	0.12
Cleaning and maintenance services	0.75	0.35	0.10
Book stores	0.67	0.24	0.12
Fabric stores	0.76	0.28	0.08
Auto parts stores	0.64	0.26	0.09
Variety stores	0.89	0.42	0.10
Jewelry stores	1.30	0.35	0.07
Mail order stores	0.78	0.17	0.07
Equipment rental and lease	0.80	0.22	0.10
Floor covering stores	0.56	0.16	0.06
Bowling alleys	0.80	0.39	0.09
Family clothing	0.91	0.30	0.08
Drapery and upholstery stores	0.35	0.13	0.04
Music stores	0.40	0.06	0.03
Women's clothing	1.20	0.30	0.02
Dry cleaning plants	0.53	0.15	0.03
Shoe stores	0.84	0.18	0.03
Department stores	0.62	0.14	0.02
Children's clothing stores	0.35	0.05	0.01
Movie theaters	0.40	0.08	0.01

[a] Taken from Department of Revenue Sales Tax Permit Computer Tapes.

Appendix Table 6. Statewide Average Number of Persons Per Store for Iowa,[a] 1988

Store Type	Persons Per Store	Store Type	Persons Per Store
Beauty shops	550	Painting contractors	4,080
Automobile repair and service	605	Photographic studios	4,104
Restaurants	608	Florists	4,142
Farm and construction machinery	938	Furniture stores	4,315
Hobby, toy, craft shops	1,084	Commercial printers	4,563
Gasoline stations	1,103	Jewelry stores	4,772
Drinking places	1,228	Home furnishings stores	4,954
Used merchandise stores	1,388	Building maintenance	4,965
Appliances and entertainment equipment	1,720	Book and stationery stores	5,618
Sporting goods stores	1,730	Shoe stores	5,912
Plumbing and heating contractors	1,850	Garden supply stores	6,158
Grocery stores	2,062	Children's clothing	6,400
Automotive parts stores	2,301	Funeral homes	6,465
General contractors	2,302	Department stores	8,646
Barber shops	2,495	Variety stores	9,739
Electrical contractors	2,651	Specialty clothing stores	9,806
Coin-op laundry and cleaning	2,683	Mail order stores	10,934
Miscellaneous general merchandise	2,891	Paint and glass stores	13,401
Building materials dealers	3,065	Mens' and boys' clothing stores	14,435
Automobile dealers	3,314	Liquor stores	14,696
Gift and novelty shops	3,332	Movie theaters	15,065
Furniture repair shops	3,337	Automobile rental and storage	16,480
Women's clothing stores	3,649	Bakeries	18,912
Hotels and motels	3,669	Shoe repair shops	20,238
Hardware stores	3,767	Confectionery stores	25,174
Carpentry contractors	3,809	Watch and jewelry repair	53,290
Drug stores	3,958		

[a] Taken from Iowa retail sales tax reports.

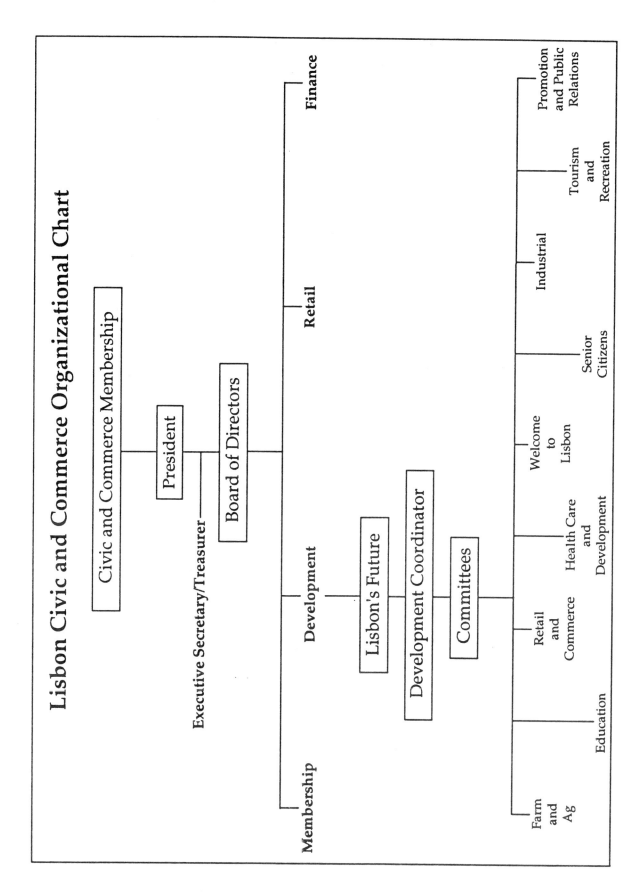

Figure 4.

Appendix Table 7. Selected Characteristics of Businesses Surveyed in Indiana, Iowa and North Dakota Towns, 1988

	Indiana		Iowa		North Dakota	
Item	No.	%	No.	%	No.	%
Types of Business						
Hardware stores	6	13.0	6	13.3	14	6.5
Drugstore/pharmacy	6	13.0	2	4.4	9	4.2
Flower/gift shop	6	13.0	0	0.0	0	0.0
Grocery stores	5	10.9	5	11.1	20	9.3
Department/variety	4	8.7	4	8.9	5	2.3
Major appliance store	3	6.5	2	4.4	6	2.8
Restaurants	3	6.5	1	2.2	34	15.9
Automotive sales and supply	2	4.3	4	8.9	13	6.1
Furniture stores	2	4.3	2	4.4	6	2.8
Clothing	1	2.2	5	11.1	11	5.1
Building materials	1	2.2	1	2.2	9	4.2
Office supplies	1	2.2	0	0.0	0	0.0
Craft shop	1	2.2	0	0.0	0	0.0
Card/gift shop	0	0.0	1	2.2	0	0.0
Convenience	0	0.0	1	2.2	10	4.7
Farm implement	0	0.0	4	8.9	14	6.5
Feed and grain	0	0.0	2	4.4	0	0.0
Farm supply	0	0.0	0	0.0	12	5.6
Other	5	10.9	5	11.1	51	23.8
TOTAL	46	100.0	45	100.0	214	100.0
Business Ownership & Control						
Locally controlled	40	87.0	37	82.2	206	76.3
Franchise	4	8.7	5	11.1	43	16.0
Regional chain	2	4.3	3	6.7	14	5.2
Cooperative	0	0.0	0	0.0	7	2.6
TOTAL	46	100.0	45	100.0	270	100.0
Years Firm Has Been in Existence						
Mean	29.4		31.3		32.2	
Median	20		27		30	
Distribution:						
Less than one	4	8.7	0	0.0	3	1.4
1 - 10	10	21.7	10	22.7	33	15.8
11 - 20	8	17.4	8	18.2	38	18.2
21 - 30	4	8.7	8	18.2	36	17.2
31 - 50	12	26.1	10	22.7	67	32.1
More than 50	7	15.2	8	18.2	32	15.3
No answer	1	2.2	0	0.0	0	0.0
TOTAL	46	100.0	44	100.0	209	100.0

Appendix Table 7. (Continued)

Item	Indiana No.	Indiana %	Iowa No.	Iowa %	North Dakota No.	North Dakota %
Years Firm Has Been Under Present Ownership						
Mean						
Median	19.5		13.9		13.2	
Distribution:	9		10		10	
Less than one						
1 - 10	5	10.9	0	0.0	10	4.7
11 - 20	20	43.5	21	46.7	107	50.2
21 - 30	8	17.4	16	35.6	55	25.9
31 - 50	2	4.3	3	6.7	21	9.8
More than 50	5	10.9	4	8.9	16	7.5
No answer	5	10.9	1	2.2	4	1.9
TOTAL	1	2.1	0	0.0	0	0.0
	46	100.0	45	100.0	213	100.0
Radius of Trade Area (miles)						
Mean	27.5		25.8		42.5	
Median	20		25		40	
Distributions:						
Less than 10	8	17.4	2	4.4	3	1.5
10 - 20	22	47.9	20	44.4	29	14.7
21 - 30	6	13.0	13	28.9	51	25.9
31 - 40	2	4.3	4	8.9	40	20.3
41 - 50	0	0.0	4	8.9	35	17.8
More than 50	8	17.4	2	4.4	39	19.8
TOTAL	46	100.0	45	100.0	197	100.0
Competitive Advantage (first cited)						
Good service						
Selection	17	37.0	23	51.1	80	38.5
Low prices	8	17.4	13	28.9	25	12.0
Convenient location	9	19.6	7	15.6	43	20.7
Quality product	11	23.9	2	4.4	0	0.0
Other	0	0.0	0	0.0	23	11.1
TOTAL	1	2.1	0	0.0	37	17.7
	46	100.0	45	100.0	208	100.0

Appendix Table 8. Customer Relations and Merchandising Practices of Businesses Surveyed in Indiana, Iowa and North Dakota Towns, 1988

Item	Indiana		Iowa		North Dakota	
	No.	%	No.	%	No.	%
Perceived Importance of Customer Relations						
Very important						
Somewhat important	46	100.0	44	97.8	212	99.1
Not very important	0	0.0	1	2.2	2	0.9
TOTAL	0	0.0	0	0.0	0	0.0
	46	100.0	45	100.0	214	100.0
Importance of Markdowns						
Yes—very important	32	69.5	41	91.1	143	70.1
No—not very important	13	28.3	4	8.9	61	29.9
No answer	1	2.2	0	0.0	0	0.0
TOTAL	46	100.0	45	100.0	204	100.0
Frequency of Markdown Sales						
Continuously	18	39.1	7	15.6	75	39.7
Weekly	5	10.9	5	11.1	0	0.0
Monthly	5	10.9	12	26.7	0	0.0
Seasonally	7	15.2	16	35.6	80	42.3
Never	9	19.6	5	11.1	21	11.1
No answer/other	2	4.3	0	0.0	13	6.9
TOTAL	46	100.0	45	100.0	189	100.0
Rating of Store Displays						
Very good	10	21.7	15	33.3	33	16.5
Good	15	32.7	23	51.1	92	46.0
Fair	10	21.7	7	15.6	59	29.5
Poor	8	17.4	0	0.0	15	7.5
Very poor	1	2.2	0	0.0	1	0.5
Does not apply	2	4.3	0	0.0	0	0.0
TOTAL	46	100.0	45	100.0	200	100.0

Appendix Table 9. Advertising Practices of Businesses Surveyed in Indiana, Iowa and North Dakota Towns, 1988

	Indiana		Iowa		North Dakota	
Item	No.	%	No.	%	No.	%
Percent of Annual Sales Spent on Advertising						
Mean		2.7		2.3		2.7
Median		3.0		2.1		2.0
Distribution:						
0 to 0.5	7	15.2	7	17.5	32	16.2
0.51 to 1.0	7	15.2	7	17.5	42	21.4
1.1 to 2.0	4	8.7	12	30.0	50	25.3
2.1 to 5.0	11	23.9	11	27.5	53	26.9
More than 5.0	2	4.3	3	7.5	20	10.2
Didn't know or no response	15	32.7	0	0.0	0	0.0
TOTAL	46	100.0	40	100.0	197	100.0
Percentage of Advertising Budget Spent on:						
Newspaper						
(Mean)	45.8		49.4		40.6	
(Median)			50		40	
Advertiser/shopper						
(Mean)	4.5		12.9		8.8	
(Median)			5		0	
Yellow Pages						
(Mean)	10.1		2.3		3.1	
(Median)			0		0	
Radio						
(Mean)	13.6		11.5		28.5	
(Median)			9		0	
Direct Mail						
(Mean)	13.4		11.7		7.2	
(Median)			0		0	
Other						
(Mean)	12.6		9		3.4	
(Median)			5		0	

Appendix Table 10. Number of Employees of Businesses Surveyed in Indiana, Iowa and North Dakota Towns, 1988

	Indiana		Iowa		North Dakota	
Item	No.	%	No.	%	No.	%
Number of Full-Time Employees						
Mean	6		7		3.8	
Median			4		2	
Distribution: 20.0						
None	1	2.2	5	11.1	50	23.8
One	8	17.4	2	4.4	39	18.6
Two or three	14	30.4	12	26.7	42	20.0
Four or five	5	10.9	9	20.0	30	14.3
Six to ten	8	17.4	4	8.9	29	13.8
Eleven or more	6	13.0	13	28.9	20	9.5
No answer	4	8.7	0	0.0	0	0.0
TOTAL	46	100.0	45	100.0	210	100.0
Number of Year-Round Part-Time Employees						
Mean	3.7		4.1		2.6	
Median			1		1	
Distribution:						
None	14	30.4	16	35.6	81	38.4
One	4	8.7	9	20.0	43	20.4
Two or three	12	26.1	8	17.8	44	20.8
Four or five	6	13.0	4	8.9	13	6.2
Six to ten	3	6.5	3	6.7	17	8.1
Eleven or more	4	8.8	5	11.1	13	6.2
No answer	3	6.5	0	0.0	0	0.0
TOTAL	46	100.0	45	100.0	211	100.0
Number of Seasonal Part-Time Employees						
Mean	0		0.9		0.9	
Median			0		0	
Distribution:						
None	44	95.6	29	64.4	132	63.5
One	0	0.0	7	15.6	35	16.8
Two or three	1	2.2	6	13.3	28	13.5
Four or five	0	0.0	1	2.2	5	2.4
Six or more	1	2.2	2	4.4	8	3.8
TOTAL	46	100.0	45	100.0	208	100.0

Appendix Table 11. Age, Education and Activities of Proprietors of Businesses Surveyed in Indiana, Iowa and North Dakota Towns, 1988

	Indiana		Iowa		North Dakota	
Item	No.	%	No.	%	No.	%
Age of Proprietor or Manager						
Mean	41.7		45.9		44.7	
Median			46		43.5	
Distribution:						
30 or less	12	26.1	2	4.5	28	13.2
31 - 40	16	34.8	15	34.1	55	25.9
41 - 50	4	8.7	11	25.0	57	26.9
51 - 60	6	13.0	9	20.5	54	25.5
61 or more	5	10.9	7	15.9	18	8.5
No answer	3	6.5	0	0.0	0	0.0
TOTAL	46	100.0	44	100.0	212	100.0
Education of Proprietor or Manager (years)						
Mean	13.4		13.2		13.6	
Median			13		13	
Distribution:						
Less than 12	1	2.2	1	2.8	12	5.6
12	23	50.0	13	36.1	75	35.2
12 - 15	8	17.4	16	44.4	67	31.5
16	6	13.0	2	5.6	36	16.9
More than 16	5	10.9	4	11.1	23	10.8
No answer	3	6.5	0	0.0	0	0.0
TOTAL	46	100.0	36	100.0	213	100.0
Proprietor or Manager is Active in Chamber or Business Club						
Yes	25	54.3	39	88.6	151	71.6
No	21	45.7	5	11.4	60	28.4
Does the Business Bank Locally?						
Yes	44	95.7	41	91.1	211	98.6
No	2	4.3	4	8.9	3	1.4
How Often Does Business Borrow Operating Funds?						
Ongoing	7	15.2	14	31.1	31	14.8
Often	0	0.0	0	0.0	27	12.9
Sometimes	9	19.6	4	8.9	36	17.2
Seldom	9	19.6	13	28.9	56	26.8
Never	0	0.0	14	31.1	59	28.2
Didn't know	21	45.6	0	0.0	0	0.0
TOTAL	46	100.0	45	100.0	209	100.0

Appendix Table 12. Experience and Future Outlook of Proprietors of Businesses
Surveyed in Indiana, Iowa and North Dakota Towns, 1988

	Indiana		Iowa		North Dakota	
Item	No.	%	No.	%	No.	%
Changes in Sales or Service Volume in Last Two Years						
Increased	28	60.9	36	90.0	83	46.1
Decreased	5	10.9	3	7.5	70	38.9
No change	7	15.2	1	2.5	27	15.0
Didn't know	6	13.0	0	0.0	0	0.0
TOTAL	46	100.0	40	100.0	180	100.0
Expected Change in Sales or Service Volume in Next Two Years						
Increase	31	67.4	25	58.1	83	48.8
Decrease	3	6.6	6	14.0	42	24.7
No change	6	13.0	12	27.9	45	26.5
Didn't Know	6	13.0	0	0.0	0	0.0
TOTAL	46	100.0	43	100.0	170	100.0
Successfulness of Business						
Very successful	25	54.3	29	64.4	92	43.2
Somewhat successful	16	34.8	15	33.3	109	51.2
Not very successful	1	2.2	1	2.2	12	5.6
No response	4	8.7	0	0.0	0	0.0
TOTAL	46	100.0	45	100.0	213	100.0
Satisfaction With Business Success and Lifestyle It Supports						
Yes	33	71.7	29	67.4	124	59.6
No	12	26.1	14	32.6	84	40.4
No response	1	2.2	0	0.0	0	0.0
TOTAL	46	100.0	43	100.0	208	100.0
Proprietor or Manager Has Used the Services of:						
Paid business consultant	3		9		37	
Small business development center	2		6		19	
Extension Service	5		13		35	
Community college	2		10		18	
Other	6		7		19	
CPA	15		0		0	